Cover Design: Prince Studio
—adapted by Jason Pollen

Interior Illustrations:
—Prince Studio
—Alan Johnstone
of Prince Studio
—Jason Pollen
—David Smeaton

For Lovers & No Others

by

Peter McWilliams

ISBN: 0-931580-01-3

Printed in USA

For Lovers & No Others

by

Peter McWilliams

ISBN: 0-931580-01-3

Printed in USA

for Bill Segesta

who kept me out of
jail back in the sixties

(does anyone remember the sixties?)

*Joy
is a word I use
to describe our
Love.*

*Love
is a word I use
to describe our
Joy.*

Part One:

How do I count on thee?
Let me love the ways.

I am
locked
within
myself.

A handful
of people
on this
earth
hold the
key.

You are
        one
of them.

I have
no thing
to share
with you
but my
            life.

I have
no thing
to experience
with you
but our
            love.

this is all.

is all enough?

help me.

show me that
I can love with
out
fears, frustrations,
falsehoods, hesitations.

show me the
face of
god.

if you
love me,
tell me
so.

if you
tell me
love me
so.

hold me
very close
tonight.

I
want you
more
than I
want my
life.

much
more.

kiss me.
quickly.

I love you.

colors are brighter
since you've come to
stay a while.

my heart beats in time
with the universal
song of love.

loneliness . . . pain . . .
where are you hiding,
my long time comrades?

maybe they have gone
where you came from;

they will no doubt
return
when you do.

Please take the
time to notice
that I am a
human being
being human,
as I not often am.

I am young,
so love is new.

There is so much
I want to know
about you.

So many things I
want to do
with you.

So many
    embraces.
So many
    moments.

take the moments:
they make the time.
take the time to see.

take the time
to make the
moment
            ours.

I (me/ all that I am and whatever I am)
LOVE (have the greatest human feeling for)
YOU (your self/you/and all that is yours)

“we haven’t
said a
thing for
an hour”

“two”

“we didn’t
need to”

“no”

“do we
now?”

turn out the light
and then
turn on the light.

Since
I
met
you,
I
have not
gone
to
bed
tired.

can you feel my soul
turn its face to God
and smile as you touch me

so

or maybe it's my heart
smiling at my love for

your soul turning to God
or your heart turning to
love

or your hand turning to
touch my face

facing my love;
feeling my God;

facing my god;
feeling my love feel me

so.

where we are
has no words.

so why do I
keep trying to
write about
It?

you,

me.

contemplate.

Celebrate.

Our Love
doesn't
have to
be
anything—

it just
has to
be.

love
&
lust
go
hand
in
hand

every time
we do.

kiss me here and kiss me here and kiss me here and
kiss me here and kiss me here and kiss me here and
kiss me here and kiss me here and kiss me here and
kiss me here and kiss me here and kiss me here and
kiss me here and kiss me here and kiss me here and
kiss me here and kiss me here and kiss me here and
kiss me here and kiss me here and kiss me here and
kiss me here and kiss me here and kiss me here and
kiss me here and kiss me here and kiss me here and
kiss me here and kiss me here and kiss me here and
kiss me here and kiss me here and kiss me here and
kiss me here and kiss me here and kiss me here and
kiss me here and kiss me here and kiss me here and
kiss me here and kiss me here and kiss me here and
kiss me here and kiss me here and kiss me here and
kiss me here and kiss me here and kiss me here and
kiss me here and kiss me here and kiss me here and
kiss me here and kiss me here and kiss me here and
kiss me here and kiss me here and kiss me here and
kiss me here and kiss me here and kiss me here and
kiss me here and kiss me here and kiss me here and
kiss me here and kiss me here and kiss me here and
kiss me here and kiss me here and kiss me here and
kiss me here and kiss me here and kiss me here and
kiss me here and kiss me here and kiss me here and
kiss me here and kiss me here and kiss me here and
kiss me here and kiss me here and kiss me here and
kiss me here and kiss me here and kiss me here and
kiss me here and kiss me here and kiss me here and
kiss me here and kiss me here and kiss me here and
kiss me here and kiss me here and kiss me here and
kiss me here and kiss me here and kiss me here and
kiss me here and kiss me here and kiss me here and
kiss me here and kiss me here and kiss me here and
kiss me here and kiss me here and kiss me here and
kiss me here and kiss me here and kiss me here and
kiss me here and kiss me here and kiss me here and
kiss me here and kiss me here and kiss me here and
kiss me here and kiss me here and kiss me here and

kiss me here and kiss me here and kiss me here and
kiss me here and kiss me here and kiss me here and
kiss me here and kiss me here and kiss me here and
kiss me here and kiss me here and kiss me here and
kiss me here and kiss me here and kiss me here and
kiss me here and kiss me here and kiss me here and
kiss me here and kiss me here and kiss me here and
kiss me here and kiss me here and kiss me here and
kiss me here and kiss me here and kiss me here and
kiss me here and kiss me here and kiss me here and
kiss me here and kiss me here and kiss me here and
kiss me here and kiss me here and kiss me here and
kiss me here and kiss me here and kiss me here and
kiss me here and kiss me here and kiss me here and
kiss me here and kiss me here and kiss me here and
kiss me here and kiss me here and kiss me here and
kiss me here and kiss me here and kiss me here and
kiss me here and kiss me here and kiss me here and
kiss me here and kiss me here and kiss me here and
kiss me here and kiss me here and kiss me here and
kiss me here and kiss me here and kiss me here and
kiss me here and kiss me here and kiss me here and
kiss me here and kiss me here and kiss me here and
kiss me here and kiss me here and kiss me here and
kiss me here and kiss me here and kiss me here and
kiss me here and kiss me here and kiss me here and
kiss me here and kiss me here and kiss me here and
kiss me here and kiss me here and kiss me here and
kiss me here and kiss me here and kiss me here and
kiss me here and kiss me here and kiss me here and
kiss me here and kiss me here and kiss me here and
kiss me here and kiss me here and kiss me here and
kiss me here and kiss me here and kiss me here and
kiss me here and kiss me here and kiss me here and
kiss me here and kiss me here and kiss me here and
kiss me here and kiss me here and kiss me here and
kiss me here and kiss me here and kiss me here and
kiss me here and kiss me here and kiss me here and
kiss me here and kiss me here and kiss me here end

Ecstasy.

say the
word aloud:

ecstasy.

shout the
word, as
loud as
you
can:

ecstasy!

softly;
gently,
tenderly,
breathe
the word:

ecstasy.

and
this
is
my
love.

you are
sleeping

I will
not kiss
you,
I will
not disturb
you.

I will
simply
crawl in
next to
you,
close my
eyes,

and
enter
your
dream.

writing
a poem
of our
love

is
like

Coloring
a
Color.

if
I
give
you
a reason
for
loving,

I give
me
a
reason
for
living.

I sit
atop
the
Empire State
thinking
thoughts
of my
love
for
you.

And the
TV transmitter
above me,
with all its
millions and
billions of
kilowatts,
cannot
impress the
Universe
one million-billionth
as much
as the
love-thoughts
I
send
to
you.

two lips
meet
to form
one kiss.

two souls
merge
to form
one love.

and this
union
is a
re-
union
with creation . . .

If
you will
help me
find as
much
meaning
in my life
as I
have found
in our love,

I know
I shall
never
die.

I am
blue.

You are
yellow.

Together
we make
green.

And
green
is my
favorite
color . . .

until I
love some
one who is
red.

Part two:

something's wrong.

missing you
could turn from
pain
to
pleasure
if only I knew
you
were missing me
too

you left
traces
of your self
all over my room:

a poem scribbled in the
margin of a book.

a corner of a page
turned over in another book.

your smell on my blanket.

where are you tonight?

in whose room are you leaving
traces?

are you perhaps
discovering
the traces of my self
I left on your soul.

I came to see you,
not the ocean.

I came to be with you,
not sea gulls.

I came to communicate with you,
not nature.

When I stare at a scene
worthy of a full color
picture postcard

I contemplate your navel

I think about you
entirely too much
while you're away.

when you're here
these thoughts I call
"love".

when you're not,
a less flattering term
comes to mind.

I don't know
whether I'm being
tested or
forgotten.

come
over
and we will
over
come
that which has
come
over
us

How long will you stay this time
I ask.

An unfair question
you respond.

An unfair answer
I reply.

in my sleep I dreamed
you called. you said
you were moving back
~~with your old lover~~.
you said you thought a
phone call would be the
cleanest way to handle it,
“it’ being that we could
never see each other
again, and that I should
understand why. the dream
became a nightmare.
I moved to wake
myself and found I wasn’t
sleeping after all.

I know it was time for us
to part,

but today?

I knew I had much pain to
go through,

but tonight

?

who took the
L out of
Lover?

run away
run and run
away
quickly
and do not
look back
ever
for I shall
consider that
encouragement
to follow run
run and run
quickly away
quickly.

iamsosorry!

Love
is indeed
that
fabled, clichéd
roller coaster.

I have written
poems of its
ups
and of its
downs . . .

But what
words can
I use to
describe the
total desolation
of being forced
to
get off
?

I have done it to me again.

No other being has the power
to hurt me as deeply as I do.

It is the "need"

The "need" for love.

I need love because
I am not happy with I;
me is not satisfied with me.

In order to stop this hurting
I must reach a point of
contentment within myself.

And that'll take
some reaching.

this longing
may shorten
my life.

Never Forget:

you were
the first
to cry the
tears of
joy.

you were
the first
to use the
word "love".

you were the
first to
touch.

and now you are the
first to want to
end it.

from first to last,
you had to be first.

ended it is,

amen.

I have nothing to continue for
for
I have no one to continue with.

I am too different to be the
same,
if sameness is love.

I am too apathetic to
care,
if caring is love.

I am too numbed to
feel,
if feeling is love.

I am too self-ish to
share,
if sharing is love.

and I am too two with
everyone to be one with anyone,
if oneness is love.

I have not anything
I have nothing
I have not anyone
I have no one.
I am not anything.
I am nothing.

and
the
tears
suddenly
turned to
laughter.

"What
the hell
am I
doing
to myself?'

"For
why?

For
who?

For
what?

what?

why?

me . . .
. . . alone?"

and the
laughter
returned
to tears.

I must
remember
that
I must
forget.

I must
forget
what I
remember.

to survive.

to forget

the
un
forget
able.

Although you are the
finest one thus far,

for the first time I feel
I would rather live
my life
alone,

than

your life
together.

So I can understand your
going,

but I wish you weren't.

And I realize why you are
leaving,

I realize, too, my hurt.

Did I love you?
yes.

Do I miss you?
yes.

Did you love me?
well.

Does it hurt me?
well . . .

it was good, and
"all good things
must come to an end."

I learned that
a long time ago.

maybe now I am just
beginning to
Know
it.

the need you
grew
still remains.

but less and less
you seem the way
to fill that need.

I am.

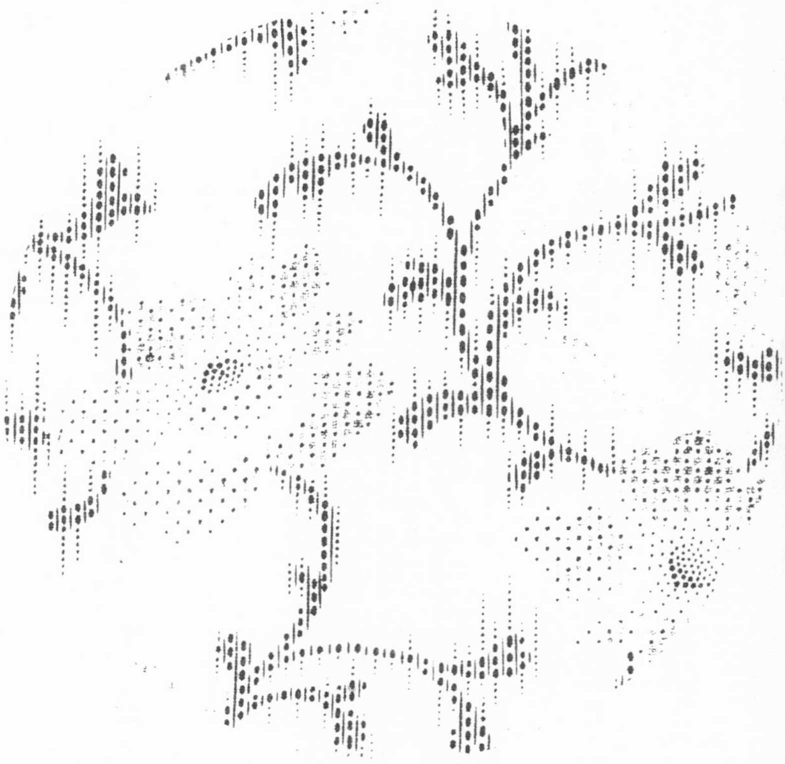

missing your love
with God's so
close at hand.

It seems somehow
a sacrilege . . .

but I think
He understands.

The books in the Peter McWilliams poetry series are:

VOLUME ONE: Come Love With Me and Be My Life.

VOLUME TWO: For Lovers and No Others.

VOLUME THREE: I Love Therefore I Am.

VOLUME FOUR: The Hard Stuff: Love.

VOLUME FIVE: Love: An Experience Of.

VOLUME SIX: Love Is Yes.

VOLUME SEVEN: Come To My Senses.

and How To Survive The Loss of a Love.
(with Melba Colgrove, Ph.D.,
and Harold Bloomfield, M.D.)

Leo Press
Allen Park, Michigan 48101

THE LEO PRESS CATALOG is more a book than a catalog. It features 60 poems, illustrated in full color, as well as information on our books, greeting cards, notecards, postalcards, calendars and whatever else we come up with. It's free. Write for your copy today.